SONGBOX

SONGBOX

poems by Kirk Wilson

Wilson, Kirk
1st edition

ISBN: 9781949487077
Library of Congress Control Number: 2021930804

Interior design by Matt Mauch
Cover photo by Kirk Wilson, "Bonobo & Company"
Cover design by Kyle McBride
Editing by Tayve Neese, Sarah Dumitrascu

Trio House Press, Inc.
Ponte Vedra Beach, FL

To contact the author, send an email to tayveneese@gmail.com.

Table of Contents

THE HALF-LIFE OF THE EMPIRE

THE NERVOUSNESS OF ATOMS

THE HALF-LIFE OF THE EMPIRE

Letter from Home

Now things change
and now they didn't

Yet we pin our hopes and so
annunciate a certain season

less certain we are kind
of an event in that the road

replaces us and if there is
support for a god in our step

In synchrony the local sparrow
is distracted for so many try

to live through it as if
it has the same charge

as the Earth and will
fall upward but

so might we shift often and
our shapes reveal a curtain

We all knew it was
a family and likely it is

best we didn't stand
arm in arm although

the switchbacks will become
more clear it looks like

the moons of a necklace
arranged in charming fans

Meanwhile you may entertain
the person you are talking

is someone else and made
of leaves when unobserved

Songbox

They have given me
a songbox

so I live on the river
where inverted illustrations

of the world's
anatomy may pass

A heron travels
just above the surface

mindful of changes
in the isotherms

and marginalia
almost written on a bridge

so insubstantial it appears
to lead nowhere

into nothing
They have given me

a story of a solitary
ecosphere where an outcast

species makes everything
anew and still is lost

And yet there is the presence
of silence in the story

they have given me
a place to sit and witness

Genealogy

In the wood I come
upon a stand

of family portraits
each a world

of inner progeny
and rooms vertiginous

keys in the shapes
of circus animals

Slowly at first
the underground

remembers its capacity
to justify a transmigration

the light changing now
and though we all

look in the same
direction we are alone

with the items
that we bring

Dispatch

I continue to observe
on your behalf

the passing days
and can report

the earth remains
the property

of empty chested
effigies

springing from
an ancient line

but now evolving
backward

The towers you remember
are now empty

many disappear
into the sand

The forests cannot
catch their breath

Plagues flare
and though fewer

birds care
to take up nesting

it promises to be
a handsome Spring

Update

Progress is slow on
the precipice

Always tomorrow's light
gleams on the tethers

and we breathe spacetime
plus remorse in every stripe

That long haired fellow in the grotto
something in his way of walking yours

something in your proximity to zero
of that understanding we have signed

The problem is our dreams are mired
so we may see the Minotaur no longer

lying in wait but only hear
his song as he undresses

his grief and how the labyrinth
itself begins to sing

and high above a polity
of oaks stands killing time

Shelter in Place

Who do I see about the price
of cataclysm

Those I know to call
have stepped into the world

behind this one and stay
busy seeking

transport to events
it seems angels love

wrestling in perhaps
the coliseum and

a pony who dances
as a formless thing

I understand
and yes I wanted

my own brief but still
I rest a mortal hope

on their indifferent splendor
fed always by the cost

On Selling My Grandfather's Farm

Dear folks although the sun remains
conventional and green jays
perpetrate the moment
the land is newly interested
to soak in more extinctions

So many have withdrawn their lives
and thus inclined not so much
from here and now but once
removed or more become
the principle of one sustained event
where things remind but empty
spaces show a curious endeavor

and mine becomes the only shadow
in that underbrush where burrows
no matter how abandoned
if you keep looking change

We must all adjust and all
I promise is I'll go on doing
routine tasks and if I come upon
the fundamental word I'll write

Meditation While Falling

The footnotes have fallen away
from the body

now attached
to bones of light

so there is something foreign
in the clarity

and the endeavor as a whole seems
per definition to yearn

in the end for spores of providence
a scheme most largely limited

to marked pockets of
vernacular exquisitely attuned

and horrified by gaucherie
preferring whole passages conceivably

opaque a context sorely needed
to make a breezy sense of chasm

and soon face or is it grasp
with something more like

notation to express
immunity to upward flight

Break Glass in Case of Plague

Meanwhile Spring
claims to come
from Paradise

and we mask up
and gods turn backs

The spoons sleep
in the drawers

The air has dusted
now we've gone to ground

Quarantine

Poison to each other
we watch the same

murder scenes
not again but again

the roads of voices
the histories

we hold underwater
wave on wave

the next echoing
the first exactly

What ancient
time has now become

the cities fortified
against a siege

the walls come down
again the air behind

the air tastes close
again like anything

is possible
and this time

everything could happen
just a little differently

Ask

Poem of moving water
poem of the beginning

poem of change
from light to leaf

teach me to read you
beyond the line

at which the distances
of objects

the breathing ones
and ones that

pray to breathe
cannot be measured

I'm asking could you
spare the words that might

anneal the nanokelvin
temperatures of souls

Debriefing

Today we hear
from an exile

who exists
in a cloud of scarcely

perceptible transition
replicated from ephemera

to express a parallel
narrative of silence

and who sleeps
with one eye open

due to the half
life of the empire

and the discovery
on the grounds

of a possibly infinite
strand of poison words

Hippo

As to a charmed place
I return

to that bright day looking
down from a dock

on the hippo who
was once a drowned boy

Meanwhile wars once young
grow old but are blessed

in children prodigious
with seed

I'm grateful for the gods'
indifference the one thing

that belongs to me
the weight of it

not weight but
its idea the judgment

of it just
since even my sins

are not original even
my fate the way it tries

to keep its mouth
shut in the shadows

Stochasticity

I make inquiries but
the words decline

to reach a nexus
committing restless

unacts now abandoned
chiefly over how

to exist in vestibules
leading one mystery

into another
These include a story

personifying distance
a monster and a question

of free will and not
even by fracturing

this stain of glass
with carnal may I

conceal the mumble
of no guarantee

lovers and estranged likewise
find themselves involved

Conjury

What is Henosis
Once the term

for mystical union
H became a trademarked cyber

platform for warfighting
a re-birth Murmur

the demon who rules Hell
once Matthias the angel

clearly understands
As a sideline M

is a teacher
of philosophy who can compel

the souls in his command
to obey the summons

of conjurers working
in the palpable

world to answer
any question posed

What is a Murmuration
M is a flock of starlings

Plainsong

Now here's aubade and
parting is so pleased to run

into more concealed
and gratified to find

existence of your limbs
and under standing kneel

Monophony

Where then the voice
of unheard music

the provost Wolmarus
writes Hildegard

in fear she crosses
the border

used to tell one part
of the composite

from the other
On this side

Wolmarus knows
remainders will

dispose themselves
in usual disquiet

maps will continue
going out of date

and all creation
will go on

trying to drive
one body into another

or transmit one impulse
through an ion channel

as if success might loose
the resonance

of some harmonic
in this world

Exosphere

I lately see
the eyes do not

have it and thus
the age of troubled

sleep more likely
to escape

intoxication and
go free

to know its lifetime
not its own

How is it
I find only

inevitable
words devoid

of myth and yet
I visit regions

that are dreams
of yours

Fortune

I make my offerings
and the mirror

makes me
in its image

of surprise
a garden

here and there
a wilderness

of deadly thieves
to consecrate

the message
of the body

afflicted with
a sense of who's

and through what
agency to contemplate

how things
persist which

no authority
can tell you

Distance

All night the door
is open

to the envoy
rich in answers

but delayed
owing to black holes

and fractal
changes in terrain

Waiting seek
the intervention

of uncertain
messages all blank

but here aflutter
as a marker

because they are
addressed to you

THE NERVOUSNESS OF ATOMS

Bones and Pennies
Pennies and Bones

Look here light falls
upon the Holocene

upon the wholly new
extinctions

This morning the sea
said to the city
I will touch you soon

This morning I tried to approach
the voice of a warbler
but the bird was calling a ghost

This morning I received
Dharma transmission
from a vase of tulips

This morning the flesh
on the Emperor's face
was too much like mine

Deus ex Machina

The light a proud horse
prances and flies

In Los Angeles
the sidewalks buckle
where the deus
ex machina has come

The children pass
as they are always passing
The light a sudden music
chimes along their skin

The aircraft speak
in the voices of dragons

The avenues end in the sea

The light a stone waits
as all stones wait
for the transubstantiation
for the word

An Act of Silence

Things shine

The gloss breathes into the soil
into the clay birds
until they rise and fly away

Another child has died at our border
in a cage

We have done everything to make it happen
and not a thing to stop it

And still the brightness rises

Our houses are so warm in winter
we are worn smooth
as the loved side of a stone

/

I found your note that says
green lights in shrub

I waste the seconds left to me

My life has proved eager
to accommodate wrong choices

All the ways I might have turned
remain outside my door unsatisfied

My house is warm in winter

I am worn smooth

The silence is sharpening its tongue

The Periodic Table

In my mother's house
a table stands
in the absence of voices

Its wood is made
of the bones of saints
and the dangerous sound
of the flute
is in the bones

But the wood is stubborn
and will make no music
without burning

It is a problem
of muscle memory from the saw
of airless space
the size of playing fields
and the nervousness of atoms

If I could speak
as the god Pan spoke
before everything he loved
was ravaged

I would say to the wood
here is the green world
Burn
Burn and sing

The History of the Future

Nostradamus poor bastard
saw me catching bullets
with my teeth

Juno taught me to hate Trojans
because she knew the Romans
they'd become

Even I can hear
something moving in the walls

I'm already disappointed in
how flat the afterglow could be
once the Messiah
has come and gone

And when I entertain my fears
for the dream of my country
my children and theirs
my neurons shine like Vegas

That's why I so admire
the guts it takes
for the mockingbird to build
another nest and blow jazz
in the spring

Make way its lyric says
for gods and seers
to come down from their mountains
and tell all right out in the open

In Quince's Play

Now I lay me down on the rock wall
that runs between my earthly
boundary
and the river of the street

The houses on the other side
are dark

Up there is the cup rim
of a moon and the few stars
a city can support

My heart never pure
is subject to the judgment
of the cardiologist

There are many things
I have forgotten and among them
is who exactly
presents Moonshine
in Peter Quince's play

Is it the tailor or the joiner
who before an audience
of one percenters takes the stage
in all courage with a lantern
and a dog

Whoever he may be I do remember
how he is cruelly hassled
but holds forth in the knowledge
that even poor players
who represent the moon
do not have to compromise
with night

Consolation

The mountain lion suffers from absence
the fox its troubles in love

The waters complain
of misunderstandings

And the distance   well
who knows

Still there is gravity
to hold wings close to the dust
there is within the light a curtain

Still those I knew when I was young
gather at my bedside in the night

trying to explain themselves
and if gods hide
within the currents of their voices and say nothing

that is right

/

And yet I am concerned about the mirror
which represents but has begun to talk
about the memories it holds of what will happen

It interrogates the stories that I tell myself

It speaks of process watching process
of uncelebrated miracles like quartz becoming sand

/

I cannot blame the past for always changing
the dead for not staying in their graves
the lives I have not lived for their resentment

the Ubers for transporting them
anywhere they want to go

In the end we must keep
communications open
in the languages
of stones and algorithms

We must need one another
as much as constellations

Lacking Metaphor I Am Alone

Sweetheart please don't you worry
I just begin
to fly in the air
J.B. Lenoir says in his
Korea Blues

These lines have bothered me
since I first heard them
as though I am Sweetheart
and worried like mad

Caesar crosses the Rubicon
and it matters or not

Nothing is clear except the correspondence
between the leaf that breathes outside my window
and the radio halo of a galaxy
that only has a number for a name

and is invisible except to certain
instruments especially the oud

Wilderness (the City)

God has told me something terrible

It can't be true

My life has never lacked in gesture

My heroes in fact are all surrealists

One was a woman who went into the wilderness with nothing
but a city around her

There is salvation in it this coming to nothing coming and asking

Asking the words even though they do not love you any more than
the thorns

/

There is this trouble we make for ourselves

Monet showed us what we can do with flowers

Please learn the flowers say

the insufficiency of all despair

/

In the city the woman wore around her everyone waited for
something to come back

It had been there once this something and waiting long enough was
the only way to bring it home

A square waited at the center where people dragged burned lynched
dismembered
other people in what must have been another time

The waiting square became an empty parking lot with ruts and cracks

and a high fence
surrounding it to keep it safe but also to keep it from running away

/

The city was not walled though through one gate came
the animals for slaughter the vegetables the tourists and through another
the diplomatic pouches and the heads of infidels

/

The light in the city was especially not sharp

This is true enough but would be different in another language

The language of squirrels or dragonflies or of a human soul in what is
    called another time

A human soul can only speak of light because it is a beast always hungry

/

The woman wore the city

There is the trouble of that verb as if anything can happen in the past

As if everything could sing once and doesn't and birds leave signs no one
    can read

What if she let the city fall around her ankles

/

The dead rise up to tell me I am willfully obscure and difficult

Look at these bones of ours they say

There is nothing to know about them beyond what you can't see

Plume

Someday maybe yesterday
we'll find a word like *plume*
out on the road
and pass through all the checkpoints
just by waving it

And by waving it
we'll wave away
the checkpoints themselves
into the light
we hope holds all things
we have waved goodbye

Eyeless Spider Denied Protection by Feds

The music that the eyeless spider hears is proof
the world exists to cognize all it's deaf to

St. Bernard tells us in his sermons
on the Song of Songs
we will not hear it in the streets

Only two he says may know the melody
the singer and the one
to whom she sings

Next

What comes after the clowns
unfurl from the enchanted
teeny weeny car

Do we discover our new space to colonize
the one without ghosts

but with very nice devices

and time erased behind us

Oh wait oh wait with time
still waiting in the bones

/

Over there's the door
the teeny wave/particle great big swallow your little
one you keep showing up at

What makes you wanta go
What makes you wanta no

Dunno dunno

/

Door mostly wants to swing

Joe is Awake

Joe Stalin couldn't sleep until the person he was having tortured had
    confessed

He knew there were sick jokes about the charges laughed at them in
    private had anyone
who told them shot in the street

The document he awaited in the bedroom where he sat smoking kept
    him up all night

But what really pissed him off when it finally arrived was it was
    ruined with bloodstains

He threw a glass of brandy at the messenger and watched how far he
    jumped

He did not want to touch the paper but took it by the edges and
    went on living for the moment
when the door closed and the messenger's footsteps could no longer
    be heard in the hall

Then he would hold the confession in both hands and feel himself
    again

Elevation

Eight billion light years under
Einstein's Cross a quasar
hidden within Pegasus
sire of Poseidon

The oak tree is afraid of it
this shiver through the air
which is always looking
for a way to feel its body

Eye level

There is something ceremonial
    about
the way the man moves with
    the leaf blower
godlike shoving noise and wind

Ground level

Prairie nymph an iris relative
flies
three purple flags

Matins

I cannot name it
that lost bird we need
to sing into the wound

Wait
I'll put my hand out for it
on the other side

THE DENSITIES OF
OTHER RIVERS

Trigger Warning: Time

I show up ahead of Time
I wait
I wait on Time
Time's up
Time's home
brushing its teeth

I go ahead and order

Time will eat anything

/

Time rushes in

The room is empty
as a hanging coat

The room is crowded up
with folks who talk
and talk and cannot quit
or they'll be turned
to taxidermied birds

Time jumps right through
the word in the beginning

Time passes doesn't
say boo

Sit down and have a samwitch Time

/

Time says in its dream
somebody's gone
and sealed it off
in its own space

where it can only see
a windowsill
and ivy in a flowerpot
and all it does is listen
to its own hooves

and nobuddy grows old
for a heartbeat or two
or wears out welcome

/

In what order Time wonders
will I tell what happens

Somebody leaves somebody

Then they're introduced
Then a husk splits
and a skinny god
drinks up the air

Time is already old
when the god approaches
in a train station
and says *I hear*

you were beautiful
when you were young

In what order can Time
tell what happens

when Time goes all the way
to the beginning
and it does not help

/

Time and me hanging out
by the river

We watch Pegasus fly over

Somebody calls out
from the other side

/

Time wants to go
fly a kite

This place is me
Time says

It's what I signed up for

Parthenogenesis going on
all over

Souls busy
as bumper cars

dozing off and waking up
a century ago
a thousand years on

Who cares if some things
are not easy to remember
and other things impossible

Who cares if the place
grows cruel or kind
with the weather

and waits its moment
on the stage
like a kid in a show
dressed up in its strange beauty

/

O Time what have you done

You must be the one
who holds my lost world captive
my animals and shiny leaves

my lead soldiers
and the friendless chairs
that adhere nowhere
except among my neurons

Somewhere I know
you keep a box in which
you have collected
like iridescent marbles
the numberless moments
I have wasted
working not to do
the work I owe

You know you have stolen
into my heart

Please
give a man a minute

I can't tell the stories
fast enough to save them

/

Hey Time remember when
we went down to the river
and the children were gathered
and we were among them
and the trees were sleepy
and the distance smoky with autumn
and the imaginary world left
nothing to imagine

and you cast your shadow on the moment
because it was its own dominion
and in it were the densities
of other rivers children trees
distances so many
it is against the rules to name them

/

Maybe you can tell me Time

Are the spirits looking back
the ones who left too soon

Do they remember the names
we made up for them

And if they look forward
what do they see

Maybe for them
you are not over yet

Maybe you have
not begun

/

Everything happens in time
but Time still sometimes
wants a body

a stalk like an asparagus
a golden eye
that opens slow and misty

maybe a scar or two
to prove its memories

the mirror of a quiet pool
or nakedness before another

Time dreams a trunk
and leaves and branches

reaches down beneath the dark
for some kind of hold

/

Time comes here to destroy
but says it's sorry

We try to explain ourselves
to one another

What if I am light
dancing on the water
I say
or a herd of aimless clouds
pushed along by the wind

You're not Time says

Time admits
there are special moments
it returns to
as though they are its children

These are the ones
so eager to accommodate
great changes
miraculous accidents
leaps of invention
that shiver through the world

Who knows where they come from
Time says
I'd like to claim them but I can't

I got a call just now
I say
another friend of mine has died

What do you want me to do
Time says
You have my condolences

/

Don't you think it hurts
Time says
to turn loose of petals
so they fall and only
start another world

If you can't see the beauty
in spiders
I can't help you

But how many froze
when I walked out on summer

The trick is
not to give them names

The trick is to take care
of your business
and move on

/

Sometimes it is an open space
with crayon sky
and animals astonished
spilling out to witness

Time says *and sometimes*
there is no light
hiding there at all

Or it may be just
a made up place

Somebody thought about
and walked away

/

Before this world started
Time drank heavily
of empty and of dark

It gladdened Time's heart
when first it came upon
starshine on the waters

and found things watchful
to observe its changes
and keep it company
until they had to go

Its favorite travel spot so far
is right here in the Holocene

It likes the insects
and going to the movies

The bad news is
even Time feels
it's moving faster now

What can be next

when the whole show
becomes a window
closing too fast
for Time's taste

/

Once I came upon Time
down on its knees
asking what it is
that permits everything

whether all Time did
in all its days and nights
was any good at all

What do I owe you Time asks
It's a pisser but
sometimes I forget

Sometimes the cities
aren't any more familiar
than the empty plains

Sometimes everything I touch
is already vanishing
before I lift a finger

/

I tell Time
I write you poems to tell you
this is how you could proceed

Find a cottage say
where you can sit outdoors
with cups of tea
and look back frankly
at the constellations

which will by then
have exited the freeway
and settled down
in their own domiciles

You do not have to stay forever
just long enough so that
the rain forests stop
exploding into fire

and birds can fly again
from one generation
to another

THE WORD REQUIRED TO SAY
THAT YOU BEAR WITNESS

Rules for Objects

Always say *Thank you* to the car
after even an unpleasant ride

To the toilet named Magnolia
Good morning

For the terrifying pencil
the telephone you couldn't love
repeatedly
I'm sorry

Carry one another heavily

Be friends

Following the funeral
of the trousers
be lost in grief for days

Enchantment as Applied to Coffeehouses

I'm a grandfather writing a line about a doppelgänger
when the glass door opens
and your doppelgänger walks in with her portfolio

To what degree does she belong to you
or you to her
I wonder as she flirts
with the barista and laughs your laugh at him

She is twenty-something

Behind her face is another which is not yours
Behind the coffee cups more coffee cups
And behind the behind
two doppelgänger children who are spellbound

Had I missed seeing them I would never have known who we were

We would have been trapped forever inside this poem
which I had never written

For Pablo

There are truths in the land
Ruthless penumbras awaken
in the midst of the most
solemn occasions

In a photo of the burial for instance
of a singularly motherfucking Colonel
the skulls of his tortured ones
trumpet like ivory around the horizon

If there is rain it slants
in the most memorable way

The landscape has its legs cocked

With a turn of the spade
the gravediggers toss your poems

fertile and capable of anything
in the picture's very center

The Visit

I often think you are only away
and while you are gone it is my work
to open up on your behalf
the door of morning
to everything that comes

I must gnaw the tasty bits
hidden in the sharp nests of bones
and listen closely to the doves
whose messages are no less urgent
for being soft
and wonder where the light is going

I am likewise charged with memory
with rising to a certain day in childhood

I cannot hear what may have happened in the night
The stones of words may have been thrown
against the glass display case of a soul
or hard news may have come

But one thing certain is the animals
were hunkered down outside the house
within great wonderments of rain
that came seldom to that country
we all would leave

Come that baptized morning
we put on our better clothes
and drove off to a visit

The rain too was traveling
to places where the land would love to see it coming
would rejoice in its touch

Strange along our way came dips in the road
like sculpted riverbeds
As if the land had formed them with a purpose
As if it wished to make the rain feel welcome

for water rushed into the beds and filled them
so full they offered to drown the travelers along their road
should any wish to go farther than this life

And we could not pass
And we turned back only to find
the riverbed behind us had meanwhile
accepted the waters into its body
and was busy rejoicing
And we were trapped as though
between one life and another

We waited in the car

I have listened
but cannot hear what we discussed
I have tasted though
the crackers and sardines we shared
and I can smell the rain

Fish Story

At exactly the same time a monster
        a catfish the size of a calf
who knows exactly what he is
        and in what he swims

(for never suppose a monster—
        and who that eats is not—
escapes the lucid trace the wonder
        of light peripheral the chink

appearing meaningless that opens
        the vista that takes the breath away
because breath becomes irrelevant)
        extends his jaws around the hook

my father a child smaller than a calf
        has cast and how they must have pulled
the child and the monster how they must
        have struggled for at exactly the same time

so much reached the distance
        of my father's life how heavily
he carried the monster who did not want
        to die for him or anyone

Fear of Fiddlers

They were thieves of souls she said
who came loud as crows
and camped at her father's gate

Their music carried on the air
like silver ash
and if you slept in it
you would no longer belong
in your life but would be lifted
to vanish on the road

(The sky was onyx then
the galaxies so close
they pulled at you)

She married young
a railroad man who dreamed
to be a farmer

By the time he had the gold
watch and the farm
the gypsy band had lost
its way in the night

Coyotes sang for her
but it was not the same

It was the violin that called
as though she had a secret name

The Photo on the Dresser

We stand there with Grace
when she was just a pup
It is the day
of her first swim

My daughter holds the camera
the husband who will be
the ex beside her

Our exes are no longer
in the picture

We wear swimsuits and smiles
My arm is around you
Grace cradled between us
our hair pasted down

The lake outside the frame
stretches to the day
when Grace grows old
and swims off
on the river of a needle

The background sky
goes farther
and it is blue
so blue

Ode to a Bed

A perfect God would make a bed
and this would be the problem

There would be the means to sail
to touch your very closest friend

and there unlock the sea chests
of yourselves to let the light in

and loose the word required
to say that you bear witness

that you are present to be wounded
in the poverty of your bodies

that you renounce the calm
and welcome the gathering wind

Still Life

We woke up naked as grapes

We lifted the blinds and there was the luminous world
some tiny portion of it living and the rest dead

and all of it there in the frame of the window
to reach for with the stems of words
we feed into the vanishing point
between ourselves

For what is beautiful about a stem
beyond the poem of its function
and what can you mean outside that comfort
of your own so thickly thin
so gorgeous in the light
so wine-bright skin

White Herons

The herons came in for the night
the canes of their legs reaching ahead
into the trees their wings
ladling air for the landing

They quarreled in the voices of frogs
shuffled for position on the limbs
one discharging another into
the blue field of the evening

Wintering here they await the call
to the lunatic dance of their coupling
at the vanishing point
where they must believe

there are still other waters
in which to construct
from imagined air the spandrel
to a next generation

The heart winters too in its season
There are rivers and moons
roosts for the night and the pull
of near-remembered distance

Beside me then you spoke of Siena
the great horse on the stage
the young girls singing in the tunnels
in a place I have never seen

We watched until transforming dark
settled all argument in its indifferent
cloak and the birds became
pale fruit above the water

Naming Andromeda

We have to believe first of all that there are connecting
arcs between the stars and that they tell a story

Then we must understand the power we have
to resurrect a life in things by giving them a name

We must admit the complication of our notion that stars take
arbitrary places due to an explosion suffered in their childhoods
and are in fact still running from the scene so quickly
none of us can think about a place they are
or a way they were at one time because everything is over
for them as it is for all of us the instant it begins
and all we may imagine is the apocalyptic radiance
they fired off in our direction when time was born to hunger

While we are here to believe the story we may suspect
what counts is not so much the stars but the space between them

Could that darkness be the reason they belong to one another

Could the core of their burning single and doomed mean less
after all than the brilliance of their connection to the whole

God

One day God
says to me

Pancho
where art thou

And what could
I say

I was in Juárez
with this angel named
Asbestos Tile

I saw in the mirror
my man-sized
size
but fear and love
still grew in me
and not so much me now
but it

I said in Juárez

Chanson d'Amour

Poetry abandons me
It is windy
I go to all the places we used to be together

I have missed the wedding and can't think why
There is plenty of blame to go around

Come dark the lights are baffled by the wind
They no longer know what kind of city
to imagine around them

This is what happens
You happen elsewhere
I dream you are singing when
you are in fact singing

In the dream the wounds I have given you
become invisible

In the dream I can measure
the distance between you and my life

Dear Poetry
Please tell me

how do you love so much
(name who/what-ever here)
if not for the allure of love itself

and what is love but its allure unknown
in things unknowable

Dear Poetry
Please come home

Together we will refuse to decide
whether to take life seriously

Together we will live in that way
you burn and keep burning

Acknowledgements

"Deus ex Machina"—*Confrontation*

"The Periodic Table"—*Soundings East*, and subsequently in
The Woven Tale

"Next" and "Joe is Awake"—*The 64 Best Poets of 2018*,
Black Mountain Press

"Before this world started" and "Everything happens in time" from
the "Trigger Warning: Time" sequence—*The Texas Observer*

"Rules for Objects"—*Eclipse*

"The Photo on the Dresser"—*Langdon Review*

"White Herons"—*Southern Indiana Review*,
and subsequently in *The Woven Tale*

"Naming Andromeda"—*Folly*

"God"—first published as a postcard by Burning Deck press

"Chanson d'Amour"—*Mudfish*

Thanks

I owe all who have inspired me, in person or from the page, and that covers a great deal of ground. I've been lucky all along. Born to a family that taught me to love words. Gifted with patient teachers. Admitted in my provincial youth to a coterie of accomplished international poets—Christopher Middleton (a treasured mentor) from the UK, Alberto de Lacerda from Portugal, David Wevill from Japan by way of Canada and London, Christoph Meckel from Germany, Tim Reynolds from the US and Japan by way of everywhere—who allowed me to pretend that I was one of them. Encouraged by the inestimable Keith and Rosmarie Waldrop, who published a chapbook of my early poems at their press of legend, Burning Deck. Humbled by a long odyssey through self-created wreckages. And finally directed by silent and invisible forces (thank you Silence and Invisibility), in ways I never earned, to safe harbor among a crew of soul mates who include not only my wife and first reader, the memoirist Donna M. Johnson, but all of our extraordinary children—Lisa, Dylan, Amber—and grandchildren—Noah, Addie, Gibson, Griffin, Frankie, Lily, Inga, Wren. They are the sun and the stars.

There aren't enough pages to hold the rest of my gratitude list. To spare the ink and paper, I'll only mention my friend and heroine Karen Russell, for her unflagging support of my work, the story goddess Joy Williams for her help and her example, and my fellow members in the Locos writing group—Chaitali Sen, Rose Smith, Ed Latson—for their ever-sharp sensibilities.

Finally, the people without whom this book wouldn't exist. Tayve Neese, Matt Mauch, Sarah Dumitrascu, and all at Trio House Press, and the sensational Swedish poet Malena Mörling, who chose SONGBOX as the winner of the Trio Award. For your own benefit, please rush out and read everything she's written, and buy all the Trio House books you can find.

About the Author

Kirk Wilson's work in poetry, fiction, and nonfiction is widely published in journals including *New England Review, Southern Indiana Review, Idaho Review, Crazyhorse, Eclipse*, and others, and in anthologies such as *The 64 Best Poets* (Black Mountain Press), *This Side of the Divide* (Baobab Press), *New Millennium Writings* (New Millennium), and others. His awards include an NEA Fellowship and prizes in all three genres. His past publications include *The Early Word*, a poetry chapbook from Burning Deck press, and *Unsolved*, a true crime book published in six editions in the US and UK. Kirk's website is www.KirkWilsonBooks.com.

About the Book

Songbox was designed at Trio House Press through the collaboration of:

Tayve Neese, Lead Editor
Sarah Dumitrascu, Supporting Editor
Kyle McBride, Cover Design
Matt Mauch, Interior Design

The text is set in Adobe Caslon Pro.

The publication of this book is made possible, whole or in part,
by the generous support of the following individuals or agencies:

Anonymous

About the Press

Trio House Press is an independent literary press publishing three or more collections of poems annually. Our Mission is to promote poetry as a literary art enhancing culture and the human experience. We offer two annual poetry awards: the Trio Award for First or Second Book for emerging poets and the Louise Bogan Award for Artistic Merit and Excellence for a book of poems contributing in an innovative and distinct way to poetry. We also offer an annual open reading period for manuscript publication.

Trio House Press adheres to and supports all ethical standards and guidelines outlined by the CLMP.

Trio House Press, Inc. is dedicated to the promotion of poetry as literary art, which enhances the human experience and its culture. We contribute in an innovative and distinct way to poetry by publishing emerging and established poets, providing educational materials, and fostering the artistic process of writing poetry. For further information, or to consider making a donation to Trio House Press, please visit us online at www.triohousepress.org.

Other Trio House Press books you might enjoy:

X-Rays and Other Landscapes by Kyle McCord / 2019

Threed, This Road Not Damascus by Tamara J. Madison / 2019

My Afmerica by Artress Bethany White / 2018 Trio Award Winner selected by Sun Yung Shin

Waiting for the Wreck to Burn by Michele Battiste / 2018 Louise Bogan Award Winner selected by Jeff Friedman

Cleave by Pamel Johnson Parker / 2018 Trio Award Winner selected by Jennifer Barber

Two Towns Over by Darren C. Demaree / 2018 Louise Bogan Award Winner selected by Campbell McGrath

Bird~Brain by Matt Mauch / 2017

Dark Tussock Moth by Mary Cisper / 2016 Trio Award Winner selcted by Bhisham Bherwani

The Short Drive Home by Joe Osterhaus / 2016 Louise Bogan Award Winner selected by Chard DeNiord

Break the Habit by Tara Betts / 2016

Bone Music by Stephen Cramer / 2015 Louise Bogan Award Winner selected by Kimiko Hahn

Rigging a Chevy into a Time Machine and Other Ways to Escape a Plague by Carolyn Hembree / 2015 Trio Award Winner selected by Neil Shepard

Magpies in the Valley of Oleanders by Kyle McCord / 2015

Your Immaculate Heart by Annmarie O'Connell / 2015

The Alchemy of My Mortal Form by Sandy Longhorn / 2014 Louise Bogan Award Winner selected by Peter Campion

What the Night Numbered by Bradford Tice / 2014 Trio Award Winner selected by Carol Frost

Flight of August by Lawrence Eby / 2013 Louise Bogan Award Winner selected by Joan Houlihan

The Consolations by John W. Evans / 2013 Trio Award Winner selected by Mihaela Moscaliuc

Fellow Odd Fellow by Stephen Riel / 2013

Clay by David Groff / 2012 Louise Bogan Award Winner selected by Michael Waters

Gold Passage by Iris Jamahl Dunkle / 2012 Trio Award Winner selected by Ross Gay

If You're Lucky Is a Theory of Mine by Matt Mauch / 2012

CPSIA information can be obtained
at www.ICGtesting.com
Printed in the USA
FSHW011231090521
81270FS